Filling
Your
Love♥Cup

*To Cathy
May your love cup
always be full.*

*♥
Kay Kuzma*

ALSO BY KAY KUZMA

Building Character (Coauthored with Jan Kuzma)
Child Study Through Observation and Participation
Don't Step on the Pansies
Guidelines for Child Care Centers
My Unforgettable Parents
*Nursery School and Day Care Center Management
 Guide* (Coauthored with Clare Cherry and
 Barbara Harkness)
Teaching Your Own Preschool Children
The Kim, Kari and Kevin Storybook
Understanding Children
Understanding Children Study Guide
Working Mothers

Filling Your Love Cup

How Love Creates Love

KAY KUZMA, Ed.D.

Published by

Box 2222
Redlands, California 92373

Revised, 2nd Printing, 1983
ISBN: 0-910529-02-7
Library of Congress Catalog Card Number 83-60606

Manufactured in the United States of America

Dedicated to
my husband, Jan,
who never hesitates to fill
my love cup

Acknowledgments

To Dan Matthews, my friend, for his encouragement and interest in my radio ministry—and for suggesting I contact Roy Naden.

To Roy Naden, my producer, whose creativity, expertise, and deadlines have made this work a reality. He encouraged me to complete the manuscript and edited the final copy.

To Lee McIntyre, my radio announcer and associate, who has given time, talent and sparkle to the Parent Scene broadcast.

To Burton Brin, my editor, who takes my words and makes them live.

To Fred Knopper, for designing the cover.

To Timothy and Eriann Hullquist for their publishing expertise.

To Esther Glaser, my teacher, for her stamp of approval.

To Elmar Sakala, my colleague, for his input into the CRAFT model and for the memories of many good times we had teaching our family health class.

To my students from Columbia Union who made CART into CRAFT.

To Donna Ranzinger, my sister-in-law, who helped me celebrate the typing of the final page and for being the first person to read the manuscript.

To Debbe Millet for typing the final manuscript.

To my church family—Dale and Rebecca Barizo, Per and Monica DeLange, Kraid and Alice Ashbaugh, and all the others—for their prayers.

To my family—my mother, Irene Humpal, my brother, Richard Humpal, my sisters, Joan Pierce and Dianne Affolter, and those three vibrant children Kimberly, Karlene, and Kevin—who taught me much of what love is all about.

And to many others who have patiently filled my love cup during these recent months—Emma Brown, Marilyn Carson, Tom and Carolyn Hamilton, Shirley McIntyre, Darilee Sakala, Toini Schobe, Donna Wagner, and all my wonderful students.

"My cup runneth over."

Contents

Preface

Have you ever yearned for some magic to turn your life around? Something to heal your aching heart, restore hope and confidence, spark creativity, motivate you to service, and somehow transform the unloved into the beloved?

Who wouldn't welcome such a miracle! You might be willing to pay a high price for its formula. But you don't have to. It's available to everyone free.

What is this miracle? Love. I didn't invent it. But I'm fortunate to have experienced it.

Whether you deserve it or not, God will fill your cup of love to overflowing, so you can fill the love cups of others.

Ah, my beloved, fill the cup that clears
Today of past regrets and future fears.
—Omar Khayyam

Life's richest cup is love's to fill—
Who drinks, if deep the draught shall be,
Knows all the rapture of the hill
Blent with the heartbreak of the sea.
—ROBERT CAMERON ROGERS

Your Love Cup

Down deep in your heart, there's a cup. Not of fine china, silver or gold. But a cup of feeling and emotion, that, when filled, makes life worth living. Borrowing Robert Roger's words, I call it the love cup.

To speak of a cup of love is, of course, a metaphor. But the picture might help you better to understand a difficult concept.

Yes, you have a love cup. Let me explain. Close your eyes. Think of a warm spring day. The scent of blossoms in the air; birds singing. No clocks. No appointments. No deadlines. No conflicts. No worries. Picture yourself with someone you love. Silence. Then that special one turns to you and whispers some kind words of love.

Concentrate on the scene for a few seconds. How do you feel? How is your love cup? Can you feel it filling up?

Surely you do, love that transforms, motivates, and inspires.

1

Much of the time we're unaware of the cup within us. We get by, existing from day to day with a partly-filled cup. When it's empty, we feel it hard and cold within, almost like we're dying. When it's full, we feel the other extreme, an all-encompassing warmth and contentment. It makes us eager to share. We want to sing and shout for joy, and we truly begin to live.

Life is for living, not merely existing. No one wants to falter from an insufficient love supply. So think about that love cup inside you. Sharpen your senses to signal you when the cup begins to empty. Fine-tune your perceptions to the feelings of others. Learn to catch their signal, "my love cup is running low."

The love cup is like an emotional barometer that can predict behavior. When it's full and overflowing, you become a loving person. It's as if your life is so filled with love you can't hold it all! You want to share those good feelings with others. But when your cup is running low, you feel unloved, rejected, and empty—you have nothing to give. When your cup is drained, your world turns negative: criticism, sarcasm, guilt, and bitterness rush in to fill the void. You have nothing but bitter gall to share with others.

Most children and many adults equate love with attention. When denied attention they feel unloved. So they seek for attention. And it doesn't take long for a child to learn a sure-fire road to get it: just be obnoxious, disobedient, or destructive!

Picture the scene. The children are playing and having a good time. You peek around a corner, sigh a parental sigh of relief and dash to the bedroom to change the beds. You listen again. All is quiet so you start the laundry. Time to confront the breakfast dishes. Then you hear wild shouting. Crash! A lamp hits the floor. Panic. Has World War III begun?

Billy screams, "Stop pulling my hair!" He aims a swift kick at his attacking sister. Mary doubles over to emphasize her pain. She started the skirmish so she's bidding for all the sympathy she can extract. She waits for you to make the scene.

Sure enough, you enter the battle zone and fall into the children's trap. The wounded warriors have your undivided attention. You pick up Mary who is suffering dramatically from that brutal kick. Her sobs are heart-rending; Billy shouts, "She started it! She started it! She called me a nerd and pulled my hair!"

"You knocked over the lamp," accuses Mary. And so it goes.

Peace is restored. Sometime later Billy feels lonely. He has nothing to do. Nobody loves him because nobody has the time to play cars with him or listen to his tale about those giants who live under his bed. Mom is helping Mary with her dumb piano lesson, combing Sally's hair, cleaning house or talking on the phone. Suddenly, action: Billy trips over the lamp cord. Crash! Again the lamp hits the floor. Again, you come running. And again, Billy is "rewarded." He has gained your attention!

Billy doesn't like the scolding he gets for destructive behavior. But he does like the attention. For children, attention—even negative—is better than none at all. Early in life Billy discovers the easiest way to get attention is to do something wrong.

Billy's attention-getting behavior is merely a symptom of an unfilled love cup. It's a way of saying, "Fill it up." Instead, Mom drains his cup further by giving him the punishment she thinks he deserves. But there is a way to break the cycle. Give Billy lots of positive attention—fill his love cup, and try significantly to decrease the times you give attention for inappropriate behavior. Then he won't be forced to seek attention by misbehaving.

Some parents object to filling a child's love cup after misbehavior. To them it sounds like a failure to "train up a child in the way he should go." But that's not what I mean. I'm not talking about how to mete out discipline. That's another subject. I'm just suggesting that an empty love cup is sometimes the cause of negative behavior. If this is true, no amount of influence, teaching, discipline, or punishment will make much difference until the cause is treated.

Therefore, instead of reacting with harsh punishment and further emptying the child's cup, first try filling his cup with your time, encouragement, and words of appreciation. See if it doesn't make a difference and reduce his need for negative behavior.

One young mother took my seminar in Understanding Children. She remained skeptical. Her five-year-old David was so unruly she was desperate, ready to try anything. For a few weeks, she patiently filled his love cup. The change was nearly miraculous! David didn't become an angel; he was still an active five-year-old; but his rebellion disappeared. Gradually he was becoming a happy, responsive, cooperative child.

But David's mother found a new conflict. Her revised

child-rearing method caused a problem with her own parents. They disapproved. They subscribed literally to the idea of "spare the rod and spoil the child." Slowly she reverted to her old habits: yelling, and spanking. David responded in kind, reverting to his old self: obstinate, challenging, and disagreeable.

Later, David's mother reviewed the seminar materials. She re-read *Understanding Children.*[1] She decided it was worth another try. In two weeks she wrote to me: "It works. Love really works. My happy, gentle, and fun-loving boy is back again. I'll never again let anyone talk me into emptying his love cup."

Erica was ten years old. Her father related how Erica was being blamed for every offense at school. Her teacher accused her of inciting the trouble-makers. She was threatened and suspended. Her grades declined. She was treated as if she had a learning problem. Erica began to call herself "stupid." The principal told her father that it might be wise to enroll Erica in a special program for children with learning disabilities. Times were troubled; home became a battleground. Erica challenged her dad's every word. Their relationship deteriorated. Life was a continual power struggle.

Finally the father could take no more. He enrolled Erica in an ungraded program. The teacher believed in the dignity of the child. She encouraged. She praised. She inspired. Erica absorbed it like a sponge; the result: she became somewhat of a model pupil. And at home the power struggle petered out. Why? Because Erica felt good about herself. She no longer needed to challenge her parent's authority in order to feel important. In turn, it was now possible for Father to fill Erica's love cup more often. In time, Erica finally had enough love to give away.

But it's not just children—the Billys, the Davids, and the Ericas—who grow up feeling unloved. Adults sometimes view life negatively. They blame God for dealing them a losing hand. They are unhappy, perhaps bitter, because their father never gave moral support, or their mother failed to comfort them, or their friends wouldn't stand up for them. They live in an alien world where no one cares. So they've learned to look out for themselves. They spend their time selfishly indulging themselves, too often stepping on others to get what they want. But what they really want is love; it seems always to elude them.

They never experience the joy of giving; they never feel they have anything to give. Their life is empty; they crave love. But their love cups remain empty because they have never learned the lesson, "It is more blessed to give than to receive." They don't appreciate the fact that, the more you give, the more you will receive.

In their overwhelming concern for themselves, they develop characteristics that make them difficult to live with and nearly impossible to love.

God can enter a life that's filled with hate and selfishness. He can change it. In a sense, that's the meaning of conversion. No one is beyond God's healing power of love. But a word of caution: filling another's love cup shouldn't be left entirely to God. God often gives us the opportunity to be His entering wedge. When a person is starved for love, he may first need to see a little love in action; next he comes to the realization that he needs it too. Then he can be pointed to the Source. If you feel empty ask God to fill your love cup. He will speedily respond. And seek out others who can be cup fillers too.

Then when your cup is filling, or full, reach out and begin filling the empty love cups of the unlovable. You may not feel loving, but no matter, God asks no one to *feel* loving. He just says, *be* loving. It's the act of love that is important. Love is something you do. And as you love, both you and the one who's cup you are filling will begin to live life abundantly!

"There are moments in life, when the
heart is so full of emotion,
That if by chance it be shaken, or into
its depths like a pebble
Drops some careless word, it over-
flows, and its secret,
Spilt on the ground like water,
can never be gathered together."
—HENRY WADSWORTH LONGFELLOW

Don't Empty a Love Cup

Without attention the love in a cup will slowly evaporate. It needs constant replenishment to stay full to the brim. So the best way to make sure that a love cup is as full as possible is deceptively simple: don't neglect it and don't empty it!

How do you empty a cup? Each time you reject a person, shame him, or humiliate him, you empty his cup. Here are some of the most common emptying practices.

Bossing. Bossy people finish last in popularity contests. Nobody likes to be pushed around.

Naturally, at times everyone needs instruction, but it can be given without orders and shouting. Parents don't have to act like drill sergeants.

Forever engraved in my memory is the day my girls and I overheard the harsh demands of a mother with her four-year-old: "Watch out! Get out of the water! Stop running! Don't talk back to me! Sit down this instant!" Finally, the mother bellowed in frustration, "I hope you fall and break your head open!"

"Wow," my girls sighed as we beat a hasty retreat, "I'd sure hate to be her child!"

"Me too," I agreed. I hate being bossed. Even though I'm fairly compliant, I seldom feel like acting upon demand. Most persons, including children, feel the same way. Ordering and bossing empties love cups.

Threatening: It's one thing calmly to explain to a child the consequences of his misbehavior; it's another to threaten him with a punishment you never intend to apply, or one which would batter him physically or psychologically.

"If you ever do that again, I'll beat you within an inch of your life," is a threat that is sure to drain anyone's cup. To voice the thought, is to increase the likelihood that someday you will carry it out. Don't say what you don't mean.

Criticizing: "That was a stupid thing to do.... I've never seen such a sloppy job.... Look at this messy room.... Were you born in a barn?" Critical words point to a child's faults. Dwelling on his weaknesses doesn't start him on the road to improvement. Instead of saying, "What a stupid thing to do," you might say, "Next time, ask me how." Being "born in a barn" is hardly a compliment! It would be far more productive to tell the child to clean his room before breakfast or forego the meal. Say it and mean it!

Ridicule and sarcasm are especially offensive ways of criticizing. "Daddy, may I come in the living room with you and Aunt Mary?" a three-year-old once asked. "Of course not," his father replied sharply. "You didn't eat your dinner and you dirtied your pants!" The father was not intentionally emptying the child's love cup, he was only trying to correct him. But ridicule doesn't correct behavior, it humiliates and demeans people into feelings of worthlessness. When a person feels that way it's quite difficult to change for the better. It takes much courage and a high feeling of self-worth to say, "I can change."

Screaming: Being screamed at has a way of making us shrink to midget size. A high-pitched, out-of-control voice—no matter the words—makes one cower. Scream, "I love you," to a dog and watch him drop his tail between his legs and slink off to a corner. Just the tone of voice we use when speaking to children can either empty or fill their love cups.

Rejecting: When a person is being ignored, he feels rejected. Parents ignore or reject by blurting out their angry feelings: "Get out of here; I can't stand the sight of you!" or "I've had it; don't talk to me for the rest of the day!"

But parents are people, too. They need privacy at times. Tell your children you need a quiet hour alone. They'll usually respect that without feeling ignored. They can understand when you need to cool off. Say, "I'm so angry, I'm about to explode. Give me fifteen minutes alone." They might say, "Take thirty if you need it!"

Another way to reject is to be so busy the child is lost in the shuffle. You fail in those regular love routines: the goodnight story, the piggy-back ride. Or unthinkingly when your child asks to do something special with you or needs your help you snap, "No."

It was late Friday afternoon. I was desperately busy taping over-head transparencies onto frames, getting ready for an Understanding Children Seminar.

In the midst of my project Kari asked, "Mommy, will you help me write a letter to Julie?"

Kari was just learning to print. I imagined her asking me how to spell "Dear". I would say, "D-e-a-r," and she would respond, "What was that first letter again?"

I'd say, "D."

"A big D or a little D?"

"A big D, Kari."

"Mommy, does it go this way or that way?"

It would take a long time to write a letter and I just didn't have the time.

"Oh, Kari," I sighed, "I'm too busy taping."

A disappointed Kari went to her room.

As I continued taping I began to read my script—my advice for other parents; suddenly, I was filled with guilt! "How can I tell others to make time for their children when I am too busy for my own?"

Before I could call her, Kari appeared at the door. She asked, "Mommy, if I help you with taping, can you help me with the letter?"

"Of course, Kari," I said. She taped a few overheads in place and then I asked her to dictate the letter to me.

It took only a few minutes, but I was saved from emptying her love cup by failing to help her.

Don't feel guilty if sometimes you really are too busy to help your child. That happens to everyone; children must learn that grown-ups have needs, too. But the tendency with too many of us is to take time for everything else and ignore our children when they most need attention. It's safe to tell a child you're too busy, after you've filled his cup so full he has enough to tide him over.

Too often, however, this is what happens:

You come home after a busy day at work. You kick off your shoes and relax. Your little one comes bouncing in, saying, "Read me a story."

"I'm reading the paper," you reply, "don't bother me." What he really needs is a bit of attention since he hasn't seen you all day; and instead he gets rejection. Few children give up easily. Soon he will try again to get you to fill his love cup. Maybe he'll pester, maybe ask questions, or maybe beat on the paper. And you'll probably grow frustrated and drain the child's cup with threats or criticism.

Fill children first; they will be better able to accept your need for quiet, and privacy.

Ask any grandparent, "What would you do different if you were given a second chance to raise your children?", and I can almost guarantee the answer. "I wouldn't be so harsh. I'd spend more time with them." A grandmother once commented, "One day you're diapering them and the next day they're gone."

Tomorrow is not likely to be the last day with your child, your friend or your loved one, but it's a day that will never come again. The years fly quickly. Don't reject or ignore. Give the people in your life the attention—the love—they need to feel filled, today.

You may have tried filling and found it's never enough. The problem: the cracked-cup syndrome. You love and it keeps leaking through. No matter how you try, the cup seems to empty faster than you can fill. Is it a problem of your loving? Not necessarily. It may be that the person has been so hurt in life that he or she doesn't know how to receive your love; doesn't know how to hold it and let it help to heal old wounds.

Keep loving. A cracked cup is no excuse to not care, respect, accept, forgive and trust another. But you alone may not be able to fix the crack. It may take a professional; a God-loving psychologist, counselor or psychiatrist, who has been trained in understanding and fostering mental health. God needs all of us to help in His loving ministry. He can work through these professionals, too. And by you having loved first, the healing process may be hastened.

Never forget, a love cup is easy to empty. So when your loved one begins to act unlovely, don't treat him as you may feel he deserves to be treated—bossing, threatening, criticizing, screaming, or rejecting. You may end up depleting his already meager love-supply and make the situation worse. Instead, try filling his love cup. You'll be surprised what a difference it makes!

"To love is to place our happiness in
the happiness of another."
—GOTTFRIED WILHELM VON LEIBNITZ

C for Care

Love is the critical ingredient for transforming children into loving adults; for changing unlovable grown-ups into lovable ones. But what is this powerful something? What, exactly, is love?

In a broad sense, love is *giving*—giving of oneself to another without the expectation of receiving anything in return. The opposite is selfishness—thinking more of yourself than of others; meeting your needs ahead of others; taking and not giving; or giving and expecting reciprocation.

In essence, love is patient and kind, not jealous, conceited, or proud; it is not ill-mannered or irritable; it forgives and forgets; it detests wrong-doing and is happy about the truth. It believes in others and is optimistic. It is long-suffering and will last forever as Paul says in I Corinthians 13.

Now if I asked you to recite love's fifteen characteristics you'd find it hard. It's a long list and tough to remember.

Yet, it's important to be aware of the components of love in order to keep your child's love cup full. Here is an easy way: Just remember five characteristics: care, respect, acceptance, forgiveness, and trust; for all the others are contained within these five. This can be your working definition of love.

An easy key to remembering this definition of love is the simple acronym CRAFT. C for care, R for respect, A for acceptance, F for forgiveness, and T for trust.

Then when you ask yourself, "Was that a loving thing to do?", check your behavior with CRAFT and you'll have an immediate answer. Ask, "Did I *care* for the other's needs?" "Did I show *respect?*" "Was I *accepting?*" "Have I *forgiven?*" "Am I willing to *trust?*"

Let's begin with an examination of the *care* factor.

Would a baby really feel love if you cooed, "I love you," but never fed her when hungry, diapered her when wet, or held her when she cried? Hardly. She might be lulled to sleep with the cooing, but scientists tell us that to a newborn, the sound of heartbeats may be even more soothing than words.

Words are wonderful, but if they're not accompanied by actions, they become meaningless prattle. A primary way to fill a love cup is to put our feelings into practice by caring for the physical and emotional needs of our loved ones. As Erich Fromm wrote in his well-known book,*The Art of Loving,* "Love is an activity; if I love, I am in a constant state of active concern with the loved person."

Care is love in action. Attitude plus behavior. It's reaching out to the helpless, the down and out; those who are in need, no matter how unattractive, sick, or obstinate.

Think about the Good Samaritan. How "good" would he have been if, coming upon the bloody man, he had respected him, accepted him, forgiven him, and trusted him, but had walked away, saying, "Sir, I'm sorry you're in such an awful state; I want you to know that I really love you."? Not a chance. The Samaritan earned the name "good" because he went beyond kindness of word, to kindness of deed. He spent time with the man, touched him, and was thoughtful in a tangible way. He cared for the man's needs.

Care as a basis of self-worth

It's not good enough to perform an act of caring and at the same time resent it. Without the attitude of love, care can backfire. It can have an adverse effect on self-worth. The way we care can be enhancing or demeaning. Here is how it works.

People feel valuable when they perceive that others accept them as competent and desirable. Sometimes, being in a state of need diminishes competency to zero. It's true with the newborn; the aged, too. Then, self-worth is determined by how desirable the person feels. This can be a time of real vulnerability. The person who gives care must make the helpless feel accepted and even desirable. If not, that person's self-worth is likely to suffer.

If the period of helplessness is brief, such as a bout

with the flu, and competency returns, then recovery from a period of harsh, unloving care is possible. But if helplessness is long-term—throughout childhood—the damage to the person's self-worth may be irreversible.

Early life is the most helpless time for children, a time when the child's sense of acceptance and desirability is most vulnerable to the type of care he receives. The way you care will either enhance or diminish a child's self-worth. But it's not easy to provide care with a loving touch when you're tired and frustrated.

Imagine it's 3 a.m.. The baby is wet and hungry. She cries, but you were with her until midnight caring for her colic, and you're overwhelmed with fatigue. You stagger out of bed and pick her up briskly. She is not comforted; instead, she screams louder. "Yuck," you grumble as you feel her messy pants. Bathing her at that hour is the last thing you want to do. She can wait until morning. You plop her back into the crib, prop up a bottle of cold milk, and stumble back to bed.

What is the baby's reaction? If she could verbalize, would she say, "Poor Mom, she sure doesn't like to be disturbed in the middle of the night. I won't cry any more. It's unfair, especially since I kept her up till midnight." Not at all! Instead, her unmet needs cause her to cry again, the only way she can call for help. If she must endure harsh or punitive care with each cry, she's unlikely to grow up thinking of herself as a desirable person. She'll probably begin to gain the feeling she's of little worth. She has small competence in her helpless infancy; instead of feeling desirable, she feels repulsive.

It is also possible for our care to blur the child's image of his competence and thus mar his sense of self-worth.

It is not loving to continue doing something for a child after he can benefit by doing it himself. This tendency to over-protectiveness takes away the child's sense of self-worth gained by successfully doing things for himself.

Our concept of self is formed as a result of numerous interactions with the significant people in our lives. If those interactions carry the message that we're competent and desirable, we believe it and grow toward that ideal. If the message is that we're incompetent and worthless, we tend to believe that, irrespective of whether it's true or false.

The concept the child forms of himself is a reflection of how he perceives others see him. So often, it is the way we care that portrays the most vivid picture. If we can care with love and respect, even when the child is disagreeable, then he begins to view himself as desirable. When you feel desirable, you can get on with the business of growing into competency.

The dimensions of care

The three dimensions of care are time, touch, and thoughtfulness.

Time. Care takes time. Perhaps that is why so many people resent giving care to others. Once the care is given, it often must be repeated again and again. You're never quite finished! This is especially true with young children.

When my children were infants—six to 12 months old—I really resented feeding them. How time-consuming it was. I'd try to slip solid food past a tongue that rejected each spoonful. Over and over, in and out, feed the spoonful, catch the rejects, again and again. Sometimes I found myself begging: "Come on, swallow it. Please. I have so much to do; I don't have all day!" Resentment was growing; I know it was etched on my face as I groaned and moaned with each mouthful that didn't go down! I dreaded feeding time.

One day I read Antoine de Saint-Exupery's delightful book, *The Little Prince*. The story was about a young prince that lived on an asteroid where he spent his time caring for a little rose—"the only rose in the world," she had told him. In time, he lost patience with the responsibility of caring for it. He left the asteroid, came to earth, and, to his amazement, came upon a garden full of roses. He felt deeply hurt when he realized his rose had deceived him. A wise fox consoled him with these words, "It is the time you have wasted for your rose that makes your rose so important."

I thought about that statement. Care can easily seem like time wasted. You may work from sun to sun but your work is never done. You feed and diaper them, knowing you'll have to repeat the same process day in and day out for months. And what do you have to show for the time spent in giving care? A trashcan full of empty baby food jars and three dozen washed-out diapers. Some reward!

Yet, it's the very time we invest in a child that pays off to its benefit. By caring, we communicate that he or she is desirable. Knowing this, the child develops a healthy self-image, a feeling of value and importance.

The baby cries; you pick him up. If your jiggling, rocking, singing, and tickling succeeds in turning him into smiles, it's rewarding to you and you enjoy the caring. But if your efforts bring on a further flood of tears, you tend to pull away and call for another person who may be more effective.

Fathers often feel ineffective; especially those who have minimum contact during the infant's early months. Early on, children begin to recognize the people familiar to them and become apprehensive of strangers. If Mom is the most familiar person, Dad may seem like a stranger. Consequently, his closeness may be more discomfort than comfort.

To Dad: If this happens to you, don't follow your first impulse. Don't call in Mom, the expert, and let her take charge while you put even more time into those things where you're really competent. Although you may buy bigger and better things for the baby, a child of any age would rather have your presence than your presents.

The best way to feel effective, and, therefore, feel joy in the caring process, is to spend more time with the baby. Care for him lovingly, even though he resists—in time you will become familiar. It doesn't take a child very long to realize that Dad can be just as comforting as Mom.

Chad was a three-year-old who didn't want his dad to tuck him in bed. It was okay for Dad to read stories and hear his prayers, but tucking in was reserved for Mommy. One night, Mommy was doing this when Dad crept quietly into the room on hands and knees. Chad couldn't see Dad; suddenly a rubber ball came flying into the crib. He tossed it out; it flew back in. The ball game laughingly ended in a bear-hug and a good-night kiss.

The next night, Chad asked for more of the same. With that, a ritual evolved; each night, the air was filled with balls, slippers, socks, and stuffed toys.

One day, a friend asked Chad, "Does your dad read bedtime stories to you?" "No," said Chad with a twinkle in his eye, "he just throws things at me!"

So, like Chad's dad, you can see how a small investment in creativity might earn some handsome dividends.

Touch. A nurse had an unnerving experience. As she began to put a blood-pressure cuff on an elderly woman's arm, the woman began to weep. The nurse was alarmed. Her voice mirrored concern. "Am I hurting you?" she asked. "No," sobbed the woman, "it's just that no one has touched me since my dear husband died four years ago."

Touch is important at every age. It symbolizes desirability; people avoid repulsive things. A baby requires a lot of touching in order to develop normally. But what about older children? As they no longer need a lot of physical care, touching them may be less automatic. I'm concerned that many older children and teenagers aren't receiving the touching they need.

Studies of teenage pregnancies confirm this suspicion. These girls often report that they received little or no touching from their fathers. Maybe they did as little kids, being bounced on Daddy's knee, thrown in the air, and landing safely in his strong arms; being carried off to bed or getting their tummies tickled with his rough whiskers. But then, something changed. Sometime around eight or ten years of age, the hugging and playing stopped. Not all at once; it tapered off. This left a void in their lives. They needed to be close to someone. They wanted to be hugged. With awakening sexuality, these needs loomed ever larger. They weren't met within the family; in time, the girls turned elsewhere. The result: a pregnancy, almost always unwanted.

Touching a child in a way that arouses sexual desire is taboo, but easily avoided. It's a blessing to put your arm around your teenager as you sit in church, to reach out and squeeze a hand in the excitement of a sports event, to give a kiss on any occasion, to rub an aching back or massage those tired feet.

Keep "in touch;" it's an important aspect of care.

Thoughtfulness. Whereas concern for physical well-being is taken for granted, concern for psychological well-being must not be neglected.

My husband, Jan, was on a business trip. The house was quiet; the children long in bed. Suddenly, I heard muffled sobs. I made my way to six-year-old Kari's bed. "What's wrong?" I asked.

"I don't have any friends at school," she cried. "Nobody played with me today."

"That really makes you feel sad, doesn't it?" I replied.

"Yes," she nodded, "I just wish Jesus would come right now so I wouldn't have to go to school tomorrow."

"I sometimes feel that way, too." I sympathized. "What would you like Jesus to have for you in heaven?"

So we talked about a pretty white colt named Nikki, and other aspects of a child's view of heaven. After a while we discussed her classmates and talked about some ways for her to become better acquainted with them.

Finally I asked, "Do you think you can go to sleep now?"

"Yes, Mommy," she replied, "but may I sleep in your bed tonight?"

"Sure," I said, "Crawl in on Daddy's side."

About an hour later, I was ready for bed. There, sound asleep on my pillow was Kari. Next to her was a little pink card. I picked up the card and read some scribbly printing: "Dear Mommy, I love you. Love, Kari."

It was hard to believe. Kari's first letter was a love note to me. What had I done to deserve it? She had called for care; I comforted her. And my reward was a precious keepsake. Tears welled in my eyes. What a sweet child. I crawled into bed, put my arm around Kari and slept next to her all night.

What had I done? I gave care, filled Kari's love cup, and it overflowed to fill my own.

Caring for the physical and emotional needs of others is a prime component of love; perhaps the most active, surely the most basic.

"All true love is grounded on esteem."
—GEORGE VILLIERS BUCKINGHAM

R for Respect

Kim, Kari, and Kevin were preschoolers. They were eagerly learning about the world. It was time for a new experience—going to the store and buying something on their own. After some coaching at home they set out for a nearby ice cream store, a quarter clenched in each little hand.

I stood by the door and watched as they made their way up to the busy counter. As they waited, some adults lined up behind them. "Who's next?" The attendant looked past the children, turned to an adult, and took his order.

A small voice piped up. It was Kim. "We want some ice cream."

The attendant looked sternly at the children. Her voice was sarcastic. "So you want some ice cream. Every kid wants ice cream. Now, get away from the counter."

The children stepped back but Kim repeated. "We want some ice cream."

The attendant ignored them. She took another order. Then another. The children were frustrated. They didn't expect this and were unsure as what to do. But they were persistent; they really wanted ice cream.

This time Kim nearly shouted, "Please, can I have an ice cream cone?"

The attendant huffed, "Do you have any money?"

"Yes," chorused the children as they held up their quarters.

"Why didn't you tell me that in the first place?" She sighed in condescension, "What kind do you want?" she asked. Her stern face soon changed to smiles when she turned to help the next adult.

The children didn't get napkins. I approached the counter. It was difficult to suppress my anger. "Thanks for helping my children!" I said to the attendant. I restrained myself from saying more. She registered shock when she realized I had overheard the encounter. That was enough for me.

As we walked away, Kim asked, "What's wrong with that lady?" I responded that she may not have had a happy childhood, or never had children around her, or maybe had trouble with unruly kids in the store. But really, my excuses were lame; there is never an excuse for disrespectful behavior.

Humans have an unfortunate way of treating with disrespect those who are weak or unlike themselves. Think about it. Adults do it to children; whites do it to blacks; the rich to the poor; Protestants to Catholics; Nazis to Jews; and children to other children, expecially those who are different. No matter what size, shape, intelligence, or color, lack of respect for a person is a wide-spread problem. It's a basic reason why so many persons have half-filled or empty love cups.

Respect and human nature

Respect implies consideration for the right of another to be unique; free to make age-appropriate decisions. Force and manipulation have no part in a respectful relationship.

Some parents think of childhood errors as sins. So crying for attention, pouting when hurt, lieing to escape punishment, ignoring a command, or making too much noise must be crushed. "Train up a child in the way he should go," "Spare the rod and spoil the child," and "Children obey your parents," are applied with abusive force. Conforming behavior becomes the goal—regardless of how it is obtained.

A Christian couple once urged their toddler to point to his navel. The child refused. Foolishly they felt it was their duty to *force* the child to obey and respect their authority. They beat him for his obstinacy. Still he refused. They continued to beat him. In the end, the battered child died from the injuries they inflicted.

Force is not a sign of respect for a child. It is a sign of disregard for God's creation. "The exercise of force is contrary to the principles of God's government; He desires only the service of love; and love cannot be commanded; it cannot be won by force or authority. Only by love is love awakened. To know God is to love Him..."[2]

It is a truism that you will find in every person what you seek. If you see people as sinful, you will find sin. But if you see them as God's creation, you will find their potential for good.

Let's respect children as members of God's creation. Each has individual needs, different abilities and a growing capacity to reason and accept consequences. Let's treat children with the dignity they deserve. Let's be courteous and kind as well as firm and consistent. Let's look for the good in the child rather than dwelling on the bad. God's salvation makes it possible for us to do this; Christ's example shows us how.

Christ's example of respect

Respect should not depend upon whether it is deserved. Christ tried to make this lesson clear in the way He treated others.

First there was Mary, the adulteress. By law, she deserved to be stoned, but Christ ignored the accusations and wrote just enough in the sand for the accusers to see that they were not blameless. When they left, Christ didn't censure Mary (as most of us would have done); He merely told her not to sin again.

Later, at Simon's feast, Mary poured perfume on Jesus' feet. Simon couldn't understand how Christ, the honored guest, could accept the attentions of a known sinner. What would it do to His reputation? Besides, Simon was jealous of the attention Mary was getting. This was Jesus' chance to let it be known what kind of a scoundrel was Simon. He could have said, "Don't complain, Simon, you were the culprit who seduced Mary. Your sin is worse than hers." However, instead of embarrassing Simon, Jesus told a story. Simon got the message; his dignity was saved.

And then there was Judas. Christ knew he was the betrayer, yet at the last supper He placed Judas in an honored position and knelt down to wash his feet. I think I would have let Judas know exactly what I thought of his duplicity. I certainly wouldn't have invited him for supper!

No matter how low they were on the social ladder, no matter how undesirable, no matter how tainted with evil—Christ always treated others with respect.

If parents just asked themselves, "How would Christ treat this child?" perhaps they would have less trouble respecting children.

Treating your child as your best friend

Would you grab your best friend by the arm and drag her through a store? Would you interrupt a friend in the middle of a job when you could wait until he was finished? Would you yell at a friend, "Quit bugging me!" when he needed your help? Would you embarrass a friend in front of others by saying her hair looked like a mop? Would you threaten a friend if he didn't drink his milk or clean up a spill? Would you bribe a friend to brush his teeth? Would you read a friend's mail without asking? Of course not, yet we often treat our children in these ways.

Erma Bombeck once said she thought she always treated her children as best friends until she put her friends into her children's shoes. "Just suppose," she reflected, "our good friends, Fred and Eleanor, came to dinner one night. 'Well, it's about time you two got here. What have you been doing? Dawdling? Leave those shoes outside, Fred, they've got mud on them. And shut the door. Were you born in a barn? Fred, take it easy on the chip dip or you'll ruin your dinner. I didn't work over a hot stove all day to have you nibble like some bird! What's the matter with you Fred? You're fidgeting. Of course you have to go. It's down the hall first door on the left. And I don't want to see a towel in the middle of the floor when you're finished. Did you wash your face before you came, Eleanor? I see a dark spot around your mouth. Don't tell me your hands are clean, Eleanor, I saw you playing with the dog! Eleanor, don't talk with food in your mouth. I can't understand a word you're saying. And use your napkin!' "

What if Fred and Eleanor were your children? You'd probably think nothing of speaking to them just like that. Yet you'd never allow them to talk that way to you. You'd never treat another adult with such disrespect. How can we be so thoughtless to children when they are often more sensitive than adults?

It's never too early to begin treating children with respect. Start when they are first born. How often has a tiny baby resisted giving up a favorite toy or ceased to wiggle while being diapered? All babies do; to fight with them is futile: it only makes them resist even more. Respect their feelings and you'll find them more willing to cooperate. Courteous treatment defuses a child's resistance. Treat a child with respect and you'll have a better chance of getting the same in return.

I once watched a woman as she courteously cared for a four-month-old infant. The baby was shaking a rattle when the woman realized that he needed a change. She didn't snatch the toy away, abruptly pick him up, and carry him to the changing table. Instead, she patiently prepared him by explaining each step. "It's time to change your diapers," she softly said. "I need to take your rattle. You've sure had a good time with it, haven't you?" She had his full attention; his eyes were focused on her face. His fingers loosened. She gently took the rattle. There was no resistance. She didn't rush the child or force her will on him.

Then she explained, "I'm going to pick you up. Are you ready?" After carefully placing him on the changing table, she went on to tell every move she was making. The baby lay motionless as his eyes followed her every movement.

I watched the scene, impressed with her skill and respect. I wondered how differently children would behave if they were treated this way from birth. Surely, the need to resist would be reduced; their willingness to cooperate would increase. I never fully realized this when my children were tiny. I rushed them along— seldom taking time to explain what I was doing. I have to suppress the wish that I could start over, but it's never too late to show respect. Why not start today?

Earning respect

Ideally, respect need not be earned. Realistically, it must. Too many parents demand respect while acting in ways that tend to make children rebel. How does your child conform to your wishes—out of fear, or out of love and respect?

Would you respect your boss if he jumped up and down screaming, "I'll fire you if you don't do as I say." Of course not. You'd fear him, and out of fear, follow his instructions, but your respect for him would be nil.

Parents who are impatient and lose control of their emotions risk emptying a child's love cup and losing their respect. Obedience is not the same as respect. If you want to maintain a child's respect, follow these guidelines:

1. Be consistent and follow through on what you say.
2. Be fair and reasonable.
3. Honor the child's individual abilities, interests, and needs.
4. Guard the child's reputation—never publicize mistakes.
5. Be courteous and respectful to others.

It is especially important to treat the child's other authority figures with respect. Children are great followers of parental models.

One of the most tragic family breakups I ever observed began with the husband criticizing and demeaning the wife in front of their family and friends. Within months, the children followed suit, hurling hurtful words at their mother. The disrespect grew; her authority was challenged at every move. Life became chaotic. After a divorce, the mother's beautiful Christian character reemerged. Gradually, she regained the respect of her children. But imperfectly. At times, her children still resort to disrespectful behavior. Bad habits are hard to break.

The flip side of the coin is that children need to be taught how they can earn respect.

At our home church, the group of juniors were regular kids: running when they should walk and shouting when they should whisper. Sometimes you could catch a trace of annoyance on the face of an older person. You could almost read the thought, "Why don't these juniors behave?"

One Valentine's Day the juniors gave a banquet for the elderly members. Each adopted one as a grandparent, they made invitations, arranged transportation, served the food and had pictures taken together. By evening's end, you could hear the oldsters saying, "I think we have the best juniors in California."

Juniors will be juniors, but in reaching out with respect and courtesy, they gained respect in return. These days their errors are greeted with a bit more tolerance!

If children want others to treat them with respect, they should act in such a way that can be respected. In doing so, this world will be a more loving place in which to live.

Respect, after *basic care,* sets the stage for a loving relationship.

"The greatest happiness of life
is the conviction that we are loved,
loved for ourselves, or rather,
loved in spite of ourselves."
—VICTOR HUGO

A for Acceptance

Loving another person is a tough job. Especially if he or she isn't pretty, good, or clever. It's a hard, but important lesson to learn to accept a person who is different or whose personality clashes with yours. The temptation is to try to remake that person before filling the love cup. Yet, acceptance—the unconditional love of others—is the basis for self-acceptance.

Family advocate, Urie Bronfenbrenner, once said that every child needs to be loved irrationally. In other words, loved without reason. Loved above and beyond the call of duty. Loved not because you have to give love, but because you choose to give it. Loved for just being himself.

Irrational love frees a person to be himself. Conditional love plagues a person. He must continually please the significant people in his life, on pain of losing their love.

Think for a moment. How would you feel if you knew

your wife wouldn't love you if you didn't get home from work at a specific time? If after 5 p.m. she would ignore you all evening. If after 6:00, she'd throw your supper in the trash? And after 7:00 she'd make you sleep on the couch? How would you feel?

About 4:45, you'd start to panic. Would you make it home on time? Going home would soon become a burden. Instead of the place you really wanted to be, home would be a place you were forced to be, whether you wanted to or not. When you did make it on time and your wife was properly loving, you'd feel that she was being nice because you were a "good boy." You wouldn't feel loved just for being you, yourself, but for pleasing her. You would wonder, "What kind of a person am I if I'm not worthy of being loved all the time?

She might, indeed, love you all the time, but by her actions you receive a different message. Therefore, you would be forced to act "good" if you wanted her love and attention.

Lack of acceptance leads to manipulation

Acceptance is a powerful manipulative tool. Some people crave acceptance; they will do virtually anything for it, even accept physical pain and psychological abuse.

A secretary once related that at seventeen she was swept off her feet by a wealthy man she didn't really like. He had some objectionable traits. But she felt sure that her charm and wit would change him for the better.

She was from a poor family. She craved pretty things, fine food and the "better things" of life. They became hers on their wedding day. But her husband remained aloof. He took her to parties, only to leave her on the sidelines while he engaged in conversation with his associates.

He told her what to wear and how to eat. He frowned disapprovingly if she reached for a second helping. When she performed to his specifications, she glowed in his attention. When she didn't, she cowered in his glares.

She became his puppet, dangling this way and that to meet his every whim. But he was seldom satisfied. He always had one more demand.

When confronted with the question, "Why don't you leave him?" she replied, "It's tough to live alone, being a single parent is difficult, and he does make a decent living!"

"Do you love him?"

"No," she answered without hesitation. "I don't! How can I love someone who can't accept me the way I am?"

The amazing fact is that she could only see his faults, when she herself was far from blameless. While he was using her to meet his demands, she was using him to meet her need for comforts and companionship. Neither accepted nor loved the other.

Many people live in relationships steeped with conditions, each using and manipulating the other to meet their own needs. Each marching to the other's tune—never fully free to be themselves. Each slaves to the acceptance they crave from the other.

Don't misuse the power of acceptance. If you love

unconditionally, your loved one can experience the freedom of being truly accepted and of being truly himself. He will never feel like a slave.

Being open and honest

The need for acceptance is often so strong that it is difficult to be open and honest with your loved ones. What about your spotted past? Would they still love you? What about your doubts and dreams? Would they laugh at you? For most of us, self-disclosure is hardly worth the risk. It is better to keep out of sight the darker parts of our lives rather than risk the rejection of a loved one. But we pay the price. We can never be fully ourselves. We can never feel truly comfortable. We can never feel really accepted as long as we must hide part of ourselves. This leads further to isolation, conflict, and empty love cups.

The wife of a dentist once told me how her husband grew distant as he immersed himself in the task of setting up a new practice. She knew something was bothering him. Each time she asked, she was met with coldness and hostility. At first he was quiet, not speaking much at home. Later he retreated to his study. He ignored the children and her. After some weeks, their communication was at a minimum. In time, he refused to sleep with her. All this time she had no inkling of what was the matter. She didn't know if she had offended him, if he was in financial difficulty, in trouble with the law, or ill with a disease. Maybe he was losing his mind. Maybe she was losing hers.

At last she could take it no longer. She overcame her gentle nature to force a confrontation. She yelled, "I can't take this any longer. Tell me what's wrong, or I'm leaving!"

With this, her strong, tall husband sat down, buried his head in his hands and began to sob. "The practice is going poorly," he admitted. "I'm afraid we won't be able to go on the long vacation we planned."

That was it, nothing more. A trivial matter by any standards. But he couldn't bear to tell her because he was afraid she would not accept him if he couldn't provide what he had promised.

The wife heaved a sigh of relief and said she truly preferred to stay home all summer and tend the garden. But she hadn't wanted to disappoint him since he had been looking forward to the trip.

A month of misery could have been avoided if each had felt sufficiently accepted to confide in the other.

Acceptance and the attitude toward authority

Being loved conditionally can affect one's attitude toward authority. A study[3] conducted at a religious university found that many students were hostile toward the university and its sponsoring church. The investigators searched the data to discover why. They found that students who were hostile usually perceived that their own parents' love was conditional. A love which was earned by being polite, getting good grades, wearing decent clothes, making beds, and the like.

Non-hostile students tended to feel their parents loved them unconditionally—no matter what they did.

How does conditional love lead to hostility toward authority? One possible explanation of the dynamics: when the students were young and their parents made them angry, they, as children, could not express their feelings. If they did, love might be withdrawn. Instead of resolving the feelings, they harbored them. With each conflict, the feelings grew. Finally, the hostility was safely displaced to authority figures—people or institutions whose acceptance mattered less than parental love and acceptance.

I wonder how the perception of conditional love might affect a child's relationship to God? There is a danger that he might perceive that God loves him conditionally, as do his parents. There is also the possibility that hostility may follow. The way parents love, therefore, can affect a child's relationship with God. A heavy responsibility to bear!

If the investigation were to ask each of the parents, "Did you really love your child conditionally?" of course the majority would say, "No. We love our child no matter what."

But it is not only how you love. It's making sure that the child perceives that love as unconditional. In fact, you might love unconditionally, but if the child thinks he's loved conditionally, his perception is what will guide his life. Hence, parents must be sure that the child gets the right message.

Why do you love your child?

It's a common question of childhood: "Mommy, Daddy, Why do you love me?" What is your answer? It's all too easy to say, "I love you because you're nice and cheerful and help me around the house—and because you get good grades." Have you ever said anything like that? If so, it's time to set the record straight. Of course, it makes you happy when your children do those things, but that is not why you love them.

In a picture book titled, *The Way Mothers Are,*[4] a little one asks his busy mother, "Why do you love me?" She replies, "Why do you think?"

In a minute the little one asks, "Mommy, how can you really love me when sometimes I'm so bad that I scream?" The mother replies, "I don't love you all the other time just because you are not screaming—so why should I stop loving you sometimes just because you are screaming?"

The little one asks again, "But, Mother, why do you love me? I know," he says, "it's because some days I'm so good." Then he lists all the good things he has done.

The mother reiterates: of course, she's pleased when he's good, but that's not the reason she loves him.

Finally the mother gives a meaningful answer: "I love you because you are my little one, my very own child. From the moment you were born I cared for you, and wanted what was best for you. So you don't think I love you just when you're good, and stop loving you when you are naughty, do you? That's not the way mothers are. I love you all the time, because you are mine."

I used this book in a parenting seminar. A mother

bought one for her sixteen-year-old daughter. The girl was surprised to find a package on her bed. She unwrapped it and found a picture book. "This must be a joke," she thought. Curious, she read it. Later, eyes glistening, she embraced her mother. "I never knew that is how you love me." It's no surprise that *The Way Mothers Are* has now found a place among her childhood treasures.

I read the book to my preschoolers. They said, "Read it again." Its message is mind-boggling. They can do anything, and Mommy and Daddy will still love them. And it's mind-boggling to realize that God loves each of us in the very same way.

How accepting are you?

Sometimes, parents' acceptance of a newborn depends on looks, reactions, physical perfection, or behavior, conditions over which the baby has no control.

My heart aches for the child who is born disfigured. Acceptance of a handicap is an uphill struggle. What about the Down's Syndrome baby, the child with cerebral palsy, blindness, or a cleft palate? Could you accept these children and love them for what they are? They need to have their cups filled just the same as the bright and beautiful babies. Sadly, they often have little chance of gaining their fair share.

Even normal children may run into an acceptance snag when they don't conform to their parent's expectations, as when a boy is desired, even prayed for, and a girl is born.

At birth, children differ in at least nine characteristics:[5] activity level, regularity, approach or withdrawal in response to a new situation, adaptability to change, level of sensory threshold, positive or negative mood, intensity of response, distractability, and persistence and attention span. The way these traits combine make a child easy or difficult to live with. For example, one who is highly active, irregular, non-adaptable, intensive, highly distractable, and negative, is not nearly as easy to accept as one who stays put, enjoys new situations, adapts well, and has a long attention span together with a positive, happy mood.

Your acceptance of a child depends also on your own characteristics, interests, or family situation. You may be very active. Can you accept a child who is "slow as molasses?" You may be dainty and delicate. What if the child is something of a bull in a china shop? You may be a perfect-pitch musician. Can you accept a child with a tin ear? You may be an economic wizard. Can you accept a child who leans toward being an auto-mechanic? If you're a homemaker and feel it's the perfect career, can you accept a daughter bent on being a woman's rights attorney? Your child may be a lot like you, exhibiting all your worst traits. Can you accept that?

Just how accepting are you?

If God, who is perfect, can accept me with my many faults and defects, why shouldn't I accept a child in such a way that he'll feel good about himself? With God's help, my actions will let him know that he is loved all the time and has no need to hide his true feelings or act in a certain way just to please me.

Accepting—loving unconditionally—can make all this possible.

> "Love forgets mistakes;
> nagging about them
> parts the best of friends."
> —PROVERBS 17:9 THE LIVING BIBLE

F for Forgiveness

It was a terrible mistake. I bashed the fender of our brand new Mercedes—the dream car we had spent what to us was a fortune to obtain! And on the first day we owned the car, I misjudged a block wall. A sickening crunch! There went the fender.

I couldn't believe it. I felt ill. Never in my life had I done such a thing. Why now?

I knew how much the car meant to Jan; in desperation I began calling for help.

"Body shop? How long will it take you to fix a dented fender on a Mercedes?"

"A week or two."

I pleaded, "It's important; it has to be fixed by 5 o'clock tonight."

"Sorry, Lady."

Shop after shop, the same reply.

I knew there was no escaping it. I was going to have to face up to Jan. I tried to think of excuses; some reason, but I drew a blank; I had no excuse. I just misjudged that wall.

Too soon, 5 o'clock neared. I was nervous. Jan was understanding—but I had never before dented a Mercedes. I implored the children: "Don't tell Daddy, I will." But they couldn't restrain themselves. They met Jan on the driveway and yelled, "Daddy, you can't guess what Mommy did!"

"What did she do?"

"We can't tell."

"Why not?"

"Because she told us not to tell you she dented the Mercedes!"

He hugged and kissed me as usual. He wasn't angry at all. He just shrugged his shoulders and said, "Accidents happen."

I wanted to get it repaired right away; Jan wasn't too concerned. He said, "There's no rush. You might dent it again and we could have both dents fixed at the same time!"

We laughed and the incident was forgotten.

That's the essence of forgiveness—accepting that no one is faultless. We all make mistakes. Why should misjudgment, carelessness, or even spite disrupt a family relationship and empty our love cups? They need not, if the person who errs is forgiven.

There should never be a doubt about whether or not to forgive someone who has wronged us. Forgiveness should not be conditional upon repentance. Complete forgiveness involves two people, the offender and the offended, but the process of forgiveness may start with either. Most often as parents or mature adults, forgiveness must start with us.

At all times forgiveness should be given freely, reconciliation sought, and the incident forgotten. But sometimes forgiveness is a pretense. There is a lot of false forgiveness being practiced among families. It's a way of undermining loving relationships. False forgiveness is pretending you are forgiving when you're really not—it's a way of sabotaging the process. Instead of filling a love cup, false forgiveness empties it.

There are five steps to complete forgiveness: recognizing the problem, accepting personal responsibility for your behavior, having a repentant and forgiving attitude, working toward reconciliation, and forgetting. At each step there may be temptation to damage the process.

Recognize the problem

If you deny the problem, it's futile to start the forgiveness process. It's halted prematurely; love can not shine through because reconciliation cannot take place. If you deny the problem, you sabotage the first step.

The deny-er is a person who, when confronted with a mistake or injustice, or asked to forgive it, denies any knowledge of the problem. "Who me? What problem? There's nothing wrong. You're just imagining the whole thing!"

Sometimes someone asks forgiveness for a minor matter. The person thought he had hurt you, but to you the incident was of no significance. What should you do? The tendency is to deny: to say, "It was nothing," but by denying, you withhold forgiveness. In a way you are telling the person who asks for forgiveness that he was wrong to be so sensitive. This makes him feel worse. It would be better to say, "Forgiven."

Accept personal responsibility

Recognize that you were at fault—at least in part. You can't ask forgiveness if you can't recognize your own error. The accuser sabotages this step. He blames others for his own mistakes.

One day, four-year-old Kevin was helping plant roses. We had just dug three giant holes and filled them with water. The phone rang. I ran to answer it, leaving Kevin to guard the holes. The temptation was too much. By the time I returned, Kevin was knee-deep in water, shoes and all.

Kevin heard me coming. Too late, he figured that shoes and muddy water were a poor combination. Before I fully realized what had happened, he said, "Someone pushed me in!"

No one was there. Just Kevin. He knew that; so did I. I muttered, "Oh, someone pushed you in," and returned to the roses, waiting to see what Kevin would do next. He splashed and stomped, perhaps waiting for my reprimand. My calm acceptance of his falsehood puzzled him. Soon he asked, "Mommy, when you were a little girl did your mother let you splash in muddy water with your shoes on?"

Kevin had no reason to blame someone else. I hadn't reacted negatively by threatening or criticizing. But he wasn't taking a chance. Almost by reflex, when he misbehaved, his first reaction was to blame someone else.

The tendency to blame another is so human. It's almost like the original sin. Satan blamed God for rules he couldn't keep. Adam blamed Eve . . . and on and on, down through the generations to Kevin blaming a "someone" who didn't exist.

Blaming someone else goes beyond childhood. Picture yourself in these common situations:

Company comes. You're behind schedule; things are in a mess. You turn to the family: "If you had gotten up on time and helped me like you should, this wouldn't have happened."

You receive a speeding ticket. Angrily, you turn to the kids in the back seat, "Why didn't you get ready quicker? I wouldn't have had to drive so fast . . ."

You trip over some paint cans you had left in the garage. Your teenager gets the blame: "You've been home all day, why didn't you pick up these cans?"

Blaming others is promoted by a punitive atmosphere where wrongs are not forgiven. Some children will do anything: lie, cheat, or accuse others in order not to get caught.

Failure to accept responsibility for your own acts is a harmful habit. It promotes irresponsibility and a self-righteous, holier-than-thou attitude.

It is psychologically damaging to live with an accuser because the accusers blame everyone, including the innocent. Once the accusation is cast, doubts are planted in the minds of others. Who should others believe, you, or your accuser? Your character is questioned. And it takes character to keep yourself from repaying evil with evil.

Don't let children succeed in blaming others; don't tolerate it in yourself. Show your children it's all right to be wrong. Everyone makes mistakes. That's how we learn. Be quick to admit your own mistakes; don't indulge in blaming others, even though you might have a case. Let your children model your words, "I should have known better." "I goofed." "Next time I'll ask first." "I shouldn't have gotten angry."

It's the big person who can own up to his mistakes. Such a person commands respect. And you'll respect yourself more when you, too, are willing to take personal responsibility.

Have a repentant, forgiving attitude

"I'm sorry." They are magic words. At least, parents often think they are. How often do parents seek them from a child? Does "I'm sorry," mean repentance? Hardly. True repentance is an attitude, more than a behavior. Saying, "I'm sorry," is not enough, unless we carry through with a genuine "sorry" attitude.

We all know false repenters. They say the magic words, "I'm sorry," often through clenched teeth and with clenched fists. Together with "I'm sorry," come the barbs—often subverbal—"I'll get you next time!" or "I'll never forget what you did to me!"

To force repentance leads to dishonesty. An irate Dad threatened his son who had just trampled through the garden to catch a fly ball: "Say 'I'm sorry'!"

"How can I?" implored the boy, "I'm not sorry, and you told me not to lie."

Forcing repentance is a sabotage of the process. "I'm sorry," becomes a ritual devoid of meaning; a magic way to set things straight. A way to avoid the steps toward reconciliation.

Don't force a child to say, "I'm sorry," when he isn't. Wait until tempers have cooled. A repentant spirit is impossible when anger and revenge dominate. When they subside, you can return to the issue, discuss solutions, and the need to put things right. For some, this cooling off period may take days.

Always make it easy for the child. Leave the door to repentance open. If you're too anxious, the child will be aware that his hostile attitude disturbs you. If he is bent on punishment, he may use this as a weapon.

It is so much easier for the innocent to forgive than for the offender to ask forgiveness. The guilty person often has real difficulty in seeking forgiveness. It's as if his cup is filled to the brim with negative emotions—guilt and revenge—leaving little room for the positive attitudes of repentance or concern for others. Sometimes, the best path to repentance is for the one who is least guilty to say, "I'm sorry." The response from the other is often, "It wasn't your fault. I was at fault." This, then, opens the door for a solution; for getting on with the important business of reconciliation.

Working toward reconciliation

Love demands glueing the broken pieces; reestablishing the relationship. One couple had a "reconciliation rug." They agreed that the first one to step on the rug and start the reconciliation process was the least guilty.

When tempers became heated, they would race to see who would first reach the rug. It was often a tie; they would fall into each others arms, laugh, and the reconciliation process was under way.

Reconciliation is sabotaged by saying, "I'll forgive you, but don't let it happen again." "You're forgiven, but I won't trust you again." "I forgave him, but now I don't want to have anything to do with him." The golden rule is the best guide. Because you enjoy having a full cup, be willing to fill another's with a full measure of forgiveness.

Forgetting—the final step

I hate to be reminded of past mistakes. I was worried that a traffic ticket would mar my previously spotless record. "Don't worry," I was told, "in three years the State of California deletes the violation." That made me feel better. In three years it would be gone. The record shreaded.

Remembering past mistakes clouds your expectations of a child. A record of misbehavior makes you expect more of the same. Children tend to live out parental expectations. It can be a vicious circle.

I know it's impossible to erase events from your mind, but you can choose consciously to ignore them and certainly not to talk about them. And God can erase!

Henry Ward Beecher once said, "I can forgive, but I cannot forget,' is only another way of saying, 'I will not forgive.' Forgiveness ought to be like a cancelled note, torn in two, and burned up, so that it never can be shown against one."

Have you ever noticed how easily children forget we have occasionally wronged them or caused them pain? I've often wondered if that's why Jesus said we must become like little children in order to enter heaven.

Let's forgive—let's recognize the problem, accept personal responsibility, show a repentant or forgiving attitude, be willing to start the reconciliation process, and forget. Forgiveness makes it possible to replace the hurt, injustice, and prejudice with positive feelings of love. It can change empty lives into full ones.

> "To be trusted is a greater compliment
> than to be loved."
> —JAMES RAMSAY MacDONALD

T for Trust

"Sure I love my husband, but I can't trust him again after what he did," a jilted wife confided. I replied, "If you can't fully trust, you can't fully love."

It's as simple as that. Trust is an inherent part of a loving relationship. It sets the loved one free to be a person, to make decisions, accept consequences, and grow toward his personal potential. You should never marry someone you cannot fully trust.

But trust has two dimensions, inextricably linked: *trusting* and *being trustworthy*. You can't trust a person who isn't trustworthy. Nor can you prove you are trustworthy unless someone takes the risk to trust you.

It is foolish to trust someone blindly. You don't hand your wallet to the pickpocket. You don't confide in the town gossip. Neither do wise parents leave the cookie jar within reach of hungry children and expect to have some left for company. Loving trust doesn't mean you must be gullible or a pushover. Encouraging someone to take advantage of you leads to disrespect.

51

The other extreme is paranoia, or at least chronic skepticism. Being constantly suspicious of everyone is just as debilitating as being an easy mark. Appropriate trust is believing in someone when you have fair evidence of trustworthiness. Sure, there is risk involved in a relationship of trust. The benefits are usually worth the risk.

Trust and self-worth

There are two cornerstones for building self-worth. First, a feeling of *desirability;* second a feeling of *competence.* Just as loving care contributes to a sense of self-worth by making a person feel desirable, trust contributes to self-worth by encouraging competence.

If a person is loved (both in the sense of care and trust) he will have the equipment to develop a belief in himself.

Trust contributes to a feeling of competence by encouraging self-confidence, independence and responsibility.

Self-confidence. When a child knows other people trust him, he tends to trust himself. It takes courage to try something new—to take on a tough task you have never tried before. It's much easier if someone says, "You can do it!" than if someone doubts, "Are you sure you can?"

As a child tries and succeeds, his self-confidence grows. He reasons, "If I can succeed in this, I can in something else." Success breeds success; his competence increases.

My mother-in-law knew how to encourage self-confidence. She believed Jan could do anything he wanted to do. As Jan grew up, his mother's trust spurred him on. His mother's confidence became the back-bone for the confidence he now has in himself. That's the way it works: confidence breeds self-confidence.

Add to this the trust in God's promise: "With Him all things are possible" (Matt. 19:26) and you have a winning combination that can overcome virtually any obstacle.

Independence. Trust is essential if children are to grow toward independence. As you become more self-confident, you attempt more things. The more you do, the more you learn. And the more you do for yourself, the less you rely on others. The result: you feel better about yourself; you develop self-worth.

Children start life dependent on others and con-trolled by others. At first, their parents make all the decisions. But learning to make good decisions takes practice. An early start in decision-making is supreme training. By the time a child is 18—legal age for decision-making—he should be well-skilled in the art.

Trust your child early to start making decisions. If not, one of two things are likely to happen: First, his inability to make good decisions will lead him to a painful trial and error process in adult life. Second, he will be unable and unwilling to make decisions, will lean on his parents into adult life, and never really cut the apron strings.

How much better to trust youngsters to make appro-priate decisions during their growing years. Let them practice early while you are around to pick them up, dust them off, and encourage them to try again.

Responsibility: A sixteen-year-old computer wizard was doing some part-time programming for the department of biostatistics and epidemiology at Loma Linda University where Jan is chairman. One day, an important package arrived at the airport and was waiting to be picked up. No one was able to leave work except the teenager. Jan asked him to drive the school vehicle and pick up the package.

Some years later, the same student was finishing graduate school. He dropped by to thank Jan for the job that started him on his career. "I really enjoyed working with computers, but the day that stands out in my memory was when you trusted me to drive to the airport!"

The process of maturing involves a gradual assumption of more and more responsibility. Yet, so often adults are reluctant to trust an inexperienced child even though he may be capable. The benefit of fulfilled responsibility is a feeling of confidence and worth. Don't let your lack of trust deny this to a young person.

Trust, once extended, is seldom betrayed. Little transgressions happen, a child may disappoint you, but rarely is it a calculated choice to avoid responsibility. Teenagers usually try hard to come through. For most children, it is an honor and privilege to be trusted and treated as an adult; the last thing they want is to disappoint.

In my college days, Mrs. Cady, the dean of our women's dorm, trusted us. There were times I could have overstayed curfew and sneaked through a window after the doors were locked. (It had been done.) But I wouldn't think of such a thing. Mrs. Cady would have been so disappointed. I wanted to prove I was responsible.

A psychology professor once mentioned to me that as a youth he had numerous occasions to take advantage sexually of his girlfriends, but he never did. Not because of willpower, but because his parents trusted him to live an honorable life. Although they no longer controlled him, their trust influenced his conduct.

A friend of mine once toured a work-study school. He was amazed to see how much responsibility the students accepted. Junior high students drove tractors. Students answered phones and prepared teaching materials. The tour leader was an eleven-year-old who had been there for two weeks after a record of being expelled from eight other schools. When given responsibility, she accepted it and received due recognition for a job well done. She no longer needed to rely on unruly behavior for attention.

Trust, self-confidence, independence, and responsibility permit the child to develop his abilities and skills.

How to trust appropriately

Some may say: "Granted, trust is important. In theory, it's great, but how can I best put it into practice? How do I know when it's appropriate to trust?"

It is sometimes difficult to determine whether or not a child is ready to assume more responsibility. But three ideas should help guide you.

First, the child, as a decision-maker, should *seek* the information he needs to reach a good decision.

Second, the child should be able to *evaluate* the alternatives, weigh the pros and cons, and learn the possible consequences.

Third, the child must be ready to *accept* the consequences of his decisions. It won't do for him to make a poor decision resulting in your (not his) suffering the consequences.

To recall these steps, simply remember the acronym SEA. S for *seek information*, E for *evaluate the alternatives* and A for *accept the consequences*.

Imagine your teenager has a piano recital early Sunday morning. She wants to attend a slumber party Saturday night. The slumber in such parties is, of course, conspicuous by its absence. Going to the party might be a poor choice for someone wanting to play her best.

But your daughter is adamant. She really wants to go. All her friends will be there.

An easy way to handle this would be emphatically to say, "NO!" and ignore the temper tantrum. But you realize something: you might deny her the party, but at home you could hardly force her to practice and retire early. She might be resentful, purposely play poorly, or refuse to play at all.

As an alternative, try SEA. First, help your daughter to gain the information she needs to make her decision. Consider, for example, the time of the party, bedtime, food (how much, how late), wake-up time, her state of preparation for the recital, and so on.

Second, evaluate the alternatives. Could the party begin earlier and not be an overnighter? Could she stay until 10 p.m. and then come home to sleep? Would the gang be willing to change the slumber party to another night? Could the party be moved to your home where the bedtime could be more carefully controlled?

Third, discuss the consequences of the several alternatives—especially those of her leading choice. Is she able to accept them?

If she attends the party, she might not be able to play well, leading to embarrassment and losing a chance later to play in the Bach Festival. Other possibilities: after a night of little sleep, will she be able to pull her fair share of the Sunday home chores? If she's sleepless, grouchy, and miserable, some consequences then could devolve upon others, affecting every member of the family.

If she misses the party, she might feel left out, her friends might conclude that her mother rules her life, or they might talk behind her back, or think that she doesn't want their friendship. They might feel that she considers music more important than themselves.

After gathering information, evaluating alternatives and understanding the consequences, she should be able to make a decision. With this method, I have often been gratified at the wisdom of my children's choices. Most of the time their decision concurred with mine. Sometimes, when different, I was pleased by the outcome—it usually wasn't a bad decision after all!

This method helps a parent to reject inappropriate decision-making. As a somewhat extreme example, you wouldn't allow a two-year-old to decide whether or not to run into the street. He isn't old enough to seek and evaluate the information; or accept the consequences. It is all beyond his understanding.

For decisions that have less severe consequences, the two-year-old might be able to make fairly good choices by use of this approach. What to have for breakfast? Tell him the possibilities. What are the alternatives and the consequences? One consequence: he must eat what he selects. If you are willing to live with his selection, fine. If not, let him know.

Children's decision making should be appropriate to their age and ability. They should not be encouraged to make adult decisions. I once heard of a mother who got carried away. She wanted her child to learn how to make all sorts of decisions; she let him choose everything: wallpaper, make of car, and where to go on vacation. The family suffered more from the consequences of his decisions than he did. Making decisions without guidelines will never produce a good decision-maker. In fact, this boy continued to make ineffective decisions into his adult life.

So just don't turn your child loose. Trust, but trust appropriately.

Lack of trust
may lead to rejection of religion

As a Christian, I feel strongly that my children should grow up loving and respecting God and enjoying the benefits of church fellowship. Roger Dudley's book entitled *Why Teenagers Reject Religion*[6] immediately caught my interest.

According to the author, the foremost reason why some teenagers spurn religion is that much activity surrounding the church is meaningless; sermons are boring and there is little for them to do.

His next point really startled me. Many reject religion because they don't feel trusted. Instead they feel that in the approach to moral issues, someone older and wiser is always making the decision and telling them what to do. Usually it is a well-meaning parent who wants to make sure the child won't go wrong; sometimes it is a church school teacher or a pastor. But the children resent being left out; they aren't permitted to think things through and arrive at their own choices. At the very least they want those towering authority figures in their lives to explain why they are exempted from making certain decisions, or why some behaviors (or types of entertainment) are off limits to Christian youth.

Only you can ultimately make the decision whether or not to trust your child. There will always be a risk and obviously you want to avoid serious errors. You don't want to allow a child to make a decision when you should be doing it, nor do you want to usurp the decision of which the child is perfectly capable. By applying the SEA model, you minimize risk. The result: a more appropriate, trusting relationship with room for a more complete expression of love throughout the child's growing years.

Shrinking the Giants

It's sure tough to show care, respect, acceptance, forgiveness, and trust to a person who has just made you so angry that you feel like biting his head off! It's impossible to conduct a loving conversation with someone who incites you to jealousy, fear, shame, or revenge. So, if you want to be skilled in filling love cups, it is important to learn how to handle the emotional giants—those negative emotions in your life.

You don't have to be a giant-killer; just learn how to cut them down to size. Negative emotions serve a very important function. When you are in danger, your reflex response is fear; it prepares you to flee, to fight, or to avoid greater danger. When someone mistreats you, anger is the emotion that may motivate you to a solution. When you have wronged someone, guilt helps you say, "I'm sorry," and seek restitution. But when you ignore the negative emotions, they grow out of proportion and become like giants, causing you or others to feel demeaned, hurt, or shameful.

Emotional giants can be suppressed, but they're too big to bury and keep hidden for long. They keep growing and force their way back to the surface. Sometimes they seem to break out in an explosion. Other times they surface slowly.

Here is a small example of a giant emotion: Imagine that your husband failed to kiss you before leaving for work. You felt unhappy and hurt as you watched him drive off. But you said nothing; you did nothing. As the day wore on, you thought about it; you remembered that he didn't kiss you the day before. You grumble to yourself, "What's happening to our marriage? He's beginning to take me for granted. What he needs is a servant to fix supper and mend socks." You usually call him at lunch time, but not today; let him call you. Noon comes and goes, and no call. You're growing furious. "How can he treat me like this?" you ask. "If this is all the attention he gives me, I'll show him! I won't even cook supper tonight!"

What's happening? An inconsequential event has mushroomed into an ugly giant filled with unhappiness, hurt, anger and revenge. Finally, you decide to withdraw. In your anger you choose not to be home when he arrives. You go out and squander his paycheck. As a symbol, you might even leave an open can of dog food at his place on the table.

But it didn't have to be that way, had you recognized the unhappiness immediately and done something about it. One thing you could have done was to run down the driveway calling, "Honey, give me a kiss!"

Almost surely he'd have stopped the car, come back, and given you a memorable kiss. Or if sprinting down driveways isn't your style, you could have called him at work and told him you'll take a long-distance kiss over the phone in expectation of double duty when he gets home.

Doing something immediately about a negative emotion frees you from struggling with a growing giant.

Parents need to learn how to shrink the emotional giants in their lives and in the lives of their loved ones. It's a must; on it depends consistent communication with our families in a loving way.

The "I feel" giant shrinker

A few simple jingles might help shrink the giants in our lives. To start:

Straight talk is what to do
If there's no giant in him or you.

If there is no underlying emotion there is no problem. You're talking straight. Without fear of upset, you can objectively discuss home finances, tuition costs, solar heating, or anything else. With disagreement, emotion often arises. Perhaps the other person is not listening. The giant starts growing. The trouble begins when you raise your voice or feel like stomping your foot. Now your feelings are involved; you need to get the emotion out with an "I feel" statement.

To shrink the giant in your life
An "I feel" statement saves you strife.

Here is the anatomy of an "I feel" statement. It has three parts: "I feel," "when," and "because." Now, let's put it all together.

Begin with "I feel" and clearly state the emotion you feel. The more specific the better. "Hurt." "Angry." "Upset." "Enraged." "Distressed." You might say, "I feel anxious."

Next, add "when," followed by the cause of the feeling. The statement might now read, "I feel anxious when you don't let me know you'll be home late."

But that's not all.

"Because" is next, followed by the reason for your feeling. "... because I don't want anything to happen to you."

The complete "I feel" statement sounds like this: "I feel anxious when you don't let me know if you'll be home late because I don't want anything to happen to you."

Here are some other "I feel" statements.

"I feel used when you leave me alone to do dishes while you watch TV because there are better things I'd rather be doing."

"I feel angry when I hear rumors that you've said things about me because I value my reputation."

"I feel fearful when you go so close to the cliff because I don't want you to get hurt."

Remember, the emotional giants of your life may have a tendency to grow so out of proportion that you lose control. Your countermeasure: a prompt "I feel" statement.

Try a nice variation. Use "I feel" in a positive sense. When your emotion is happiness, joy or relief, let it come out.

> "I feel happy when you fill the gas tank because it saves me time and I'm off to a quick start."

> "I feel joyful when you practice without being reminded because I want you to feel joy in your music."

> "I feel relieved when the house is clean because I'm not preoccupied about the tasks waiting to be done."

"I feel" statements provide a means to communicate frankly with our loved ones or associates. It's a way to let them know clearly what's going on inside.

A word of caution. "I feel" must be followed by the emotion, not by "that." If you say "I feel that," you are giving an opinion and not expressing an emotion.

The "you feel" giant shrinker

The complement of "I feel" is "you feel." A "you feel" statement is used to deal with someone else's emotion.

When the giant's curve is thrown your way,
A "you feel" statement is what to say.

When someone gives vent to an underlying emotion, you can respond with a "you feel" statement. Examples calling for such a response: "I hate my teacher." "I never again want to walk home alone." "You're always buying something for yourself and never for me."

The emotion should first be dealt with in order to uncover the person's underlying meaning. A "you feel" statement can help to do this. Validate the person's feelings without being threatening. It's impossible to solve problems when emotional giants are sparring with one another. Once you have shrunk the other's giant with "you feel," you can continue listening until you uncover the real problem.

When you hear a child say, "I hate my teacher," you might respond, "Wow, *you feel* angry," and then listen as he unloads his emotional giant.

When you hear, "I never again want to walk home alone," you might assume fear is the cause. Children sometimes deny this feeling because it's not "grown-up" to be afraid. Let them know that fear is O.K. Help them talk about it by saying, "It sounds as if something frightened you. Tell me about it. How do *you feel?*"

When a child says, "You're always buying something for yourself and never anything for me," it sounds like he is feeling jealous, hurt, or neglected. The tone of voice may help you decide which emotion it is. Try one; if you're not correct, he will correct you by saying, perhaps, "No, I'm not jealous. It's just that I'd like to get a present, too." Your "you feel jealous" statement, even incorrect, served the purpose of encouraging the child to talk more about the problem, thus leading to a solution.

The "warm fuzzy" giant shrinker

How do you respond to people who try to put you down with malice or spite? They usually have a giant negative emotion that is moving them to action. They may be terribly upset, beyond the reach of a "you feel" statement. So try something else to shrink the giant:

If you feel put down by a giant's attack,
Send three warm fuzzies and you'll pay him back.

Warm fuzzies is a term often used for compliments, words of appreciation, or kind acts. To an agitated person, warm fuzzies work like shock therapy. A warm fuzzy is the last thing an angry person expects. It disarms him and often defuses an explosive situation.

It may not cut the giant down to size, but it keeps him from growing larger. It's also a great protection against letting your own giant grow in response to a put-down.

You come home late and your wife has been waiting supper. This is the third night in a row. Her patience runs out. She's angry and yells, "Why can't you be home on time?"

You know she's mad. And your excuse is poor. You could try a "you feel" statement; to her towering giant, it might sound like a put-down and make her even more furious. So try some warm fuzzies.

You might say, "I appreciate your having a great supper ready for me." "You're a super wife." "Supper smells scrumptious." "And since you've worked so hard, I'll be happy to do the dishes tonight." Then you should add, "By the way, I'm sure sorry. I lost track of time. I'll try to be more careful. I know how you feel. Forgive me."

It's a calloused wife that wouldn't forgive a husband after that recital. Some wives would nearly faint. After the fuzzies do their job, you can do some problem-solving without those emotional giants getting in the way.

If you wonder about the warm fuzzies, ponder Proverbs 25:21-22. Warm fuzzies are merely an application of the Biblical admonition, "If an enemy is hungry, give him food. If he is thirsty, give him a drink— for you shall be heaping coals of fire on his head." The *Living Bible* reads, "This will make him feel ashamed of himself."

If a fuzzy is good treatment for an enemy, it might even be better for a loved one. I always welcome a few warm fuzzies; I'd like to get one right now. You don't have to wait for those giants to appear!

Loving When You're Low

Love is easy to talk about, but difficult to practice. In theory, we live so close to the Lord that His love sustains us every hour of the day. In practice, we don't. On many days our ebullient highs are followed by melancholy lows. We soon find ourselves acting out those negative feelings. Some fluctuate noticeably between moods. But remember you can be loving when low by learning how to control your love cup when it's nearly empty.

Being loving is easy when things go well. What do you do when the six-year-old uses a marking pen to practice his alphabet on a freshly painted wall? You spend an hour scrubbing the paint off the wall. Marker ink, you know, is much more durable than paint. The job is almost done; you check your watch. Oops! Hurry, you'll be late for an appointment. You dash into the bedroom to find the clothes you need in a rumpled heap on the floor of the closet. Your teenage daughter has been going through your wardrobe again. Your anger is

mounting. You yell, "Pick up these clothes immediately!" The response: silence. The culprit has myste-
riously disappeared. Then you notice broken china on
the floor. The antique vase! You've had it! You confront
your toddler. Her response: "Dog did it." No repentance. Is your anger bringing you close to the breaking
point? You bet it is!

Back to our metaphorical love cup. In a sense, we are
emotional containers. We can hold only so much.
When anger increases, other emotions decrease. Love
is usually the emotion to go first. Just when you need it
most, you look into your love cup and find it drained.

You cannot control sudden emotion. Your body was
designed to react emotionally to various circumstances. But
if you are perceptive, you can control the negative
before it rages out of control.

When you realize your love cup is low, its contents
being displaced by other emotions, try these steps:

First, admit you are low. There is nothing wrong with
being low. Staying there is the problem. That's when
you become depressed and begin to deal with others in
an unloving way. Remember, you have the power to
refill an empty love cup.

Second. Not every problem needs to be handled
immediately. In fact, most problems are handled better
after you gain control. No amount of ranting and raving
can put the vase back together again. If you feel ready to
explode with words and actions guaranteed to empty
someone else, you need to move immediately to the
third step.

Third. Do something to refill your own cup of love.
Take time for a word of prayer; contact the Master cup

filler. Contact a family member or friend who makes you feel warm inside. Force yourself to reach out and do something loving for someone, anyone, and you'll feel better. Any of these things will help. When I'm really low, I try them all.

Read God's Word. The Bible has help for every occasion. When I gain insight into the reason for my empty cup, I look for God's promises concerning that problem. Here are some of my favorite promises:

> When I'm *agitated* and need *peace:* Isa. 32:17; John 14:27; Prov. 3:24; Phil. 4:7.
>
> When I'm *impatient* and need *patience:* Eccl. 3:1-9; Ps. 37:7,9; Ps. 27:14; Ps. 40:1-3.
>
> When I'm *angry* and need *control:* Ps. 37:8; Rom. 12:14-21; Prov. 15:1; Prov. 19:11; Matt. 5:23-24; James 1:19-20.
>
> When I'm *insulted* and need to *forgive:* Matt. 5:10-12; Matt. 5:44-45; Prov. 25:21-22; Matt. 18:15.
>
> When I'm *jealous* and need to *accept:* Ps. 49:16-17; James 3:14-16.
>
> When I'm *discouraged* and need *hope:* John 14:1-4; Joshua 1:9; James 1:12; Phil. 4:12-13; Ps. 34:17; John 15:9-11; Prov. 16:20; Job 11:16-19.
>
> When I'm *worried* and need *reassurance:* Ps. 126:5-6; Phil. 4:19; Isa. 26:3-4; Luke 12:22-28.
>
> When I'm *sad* and need *comfort:* Matt. 5:4; Ps. 34:18.
>
> When I'm *lonely* and need *support:* Isa. 54:10; John 14:18.
>
> When I'm *fearful* and need *protection:* Isa. 41:10; Matt. 10:29-31; Ps. 112:7; Prov. 18:10; Rom. 8:31-32; Isa. 41:13; Heb. 13:6; Prov. 1:33; Ps. 4:8; Ps. 46:1; I Pet. 3:13-15; Ps. 32:7; Isa. 43:2.

When I'm *tired* and need *rest:* Isa. 40:31;
Matt. 11:28-30.
 When I'm *sick* and need *healing:* Ps. 4:3; Ps.
103:2-3; Mark 9:23; Ex. 23:25; 2 Cor. 4:17; 2
Cor. 12:7-10; 1 Pet. 5:10; Jer. 30:17a.
 When I'm *tempted* and need *strength:* 1
Cor. 10:13; Mark 14:38; Ps. 55:22; James 4:7;
Heb. 2:18.
 When I'm *guilty* and need *forgiveness:* Isa.
44:22; Isa. 1:18; Ps. 103:12; 1 John 1:9; Ps.
51:17; Eph. 1:7-8.
 When I'm *confused* and need *direction:* Ps.
16:7-8; Isa. 30:21; Isa. 42:16; Ps. 25:9-10; Ps.
119:105; Prov. 3:16; Micah 6:8.
 When I *doubt* and need *faith:* Matt. 7:7-8;
Matt. 21:22; Jer. 33:3.

Sometimes I can't identify the cause of my emp-
tiness. Then I follow another plan. I need prayer and
support so I pick up my modern translation Bible and
turn to Ephesians 3:17-19 and read over and over, "May
your roots go down deep into the soil of God's
marvelous love...until you are filled up with God
himself." (*The Living Bible*)

 I read Paul's prayer as if I were a first century Ephesian;
as if it were written especially for me. I try to envision
how high, wide, and deep God's love really is. I reach
the conclusion that I've sealed the cover on tightly.
That's what's keeping my cup from receiving His all-
encompassing love.

 The next thing is to turn to the 23rd Psalm, my favorite
since childhood. I read about the wonderful things my
shepherd has done for me and is doing for me right
now. I repeat the chapter by memory and go back to
savor every phrase—especially the words, "My cup

runneth over"—the phrase that inspired this book. It leads me to think, if all these things are true, I have no business feeling low. So, I pray, "You've filled my cup in the past, so please, God, fill it now."

Then, when I'm refilled with love, I can shout in joy and exclaim: "Surely goodness and mercy shall follow me all the days of my life; and I will dwell in the house of the Lord for ever!"

After pondering the 23rd Psalm, I might turn to Proverbs 31. Sometimes when I read the whole chapter about the good wife, I feel a little guilty for not having worked late into the night, or for having overslept. I'm obviously not the perfect woman of the Proverbs! I have my limitations. The woman of valor is a composite of all the good in women. Although I'll never be like her, I identify with Proverbs 31:29 when I do the things God has for me to do. I even read my name into the text. "Many daughters have done virtuously, but you, Kay Kuzma, excellest them all."

Does that sound bold, self-righteous? It's not my own compliment; it's the word of God. And I know that if I could actually hear Him, those words would be His for me. But not only for me, also for you. He made us and loves each of us supremely. I'm sure it is the will of our Creator and Redeemer that we think highly of His creation! In God's sight each of us is to excell in the · tasks and responsibilities God has given us to do.

My advice is this: whenever you have trouble facing the person in the mirror, strengthen yourself with God's words of Proverbs 31:29. Do it again and again. God will fill your cup. Women, let Him speak these words to you. Men, delete the wo-, and this verse applies also to you! Consider the gifts God has given to you. Focus on your strengths; the positives in your life.

Finally, I turn to Philippians 4:4 and read, "Rejoice in the Lord always: and again I say, Rejoice." If Paul could rejoice in a Roman dungeon, surely I can find something in my world to thank God for and rejoice about. Read on. Philippians 4:8 is wonderful advice for filling your love cup. "Finally, brethren, whatsoever things are true, whatsoever things are honest, whatsoever things are just, whatsoever things are pure, whatsoever things are lovely, whatsoever things are of good report; if there by any virtue, and if there be any praise, think on these things."

Ask for a warm feeling and a prayer. I love to feel warm inside. That's my feeling when someone fills my love cup. God has helpers who are pleased to do some filling. But often they don't know whose cup needs filling. If I have a need, it's my responsibility to let them know: "I'm empty." No one has ever turned me down when I've asked. There's been some mumbling and fumbling and, "Tell me what to do," but the spirit was always one of wanting to help. So, when I'm low, I contact someone who can encourage me.

I'm especially blessed because God provided me with a husband who's a born cup-filler. Most mornings his greeting is, "It's a beautiful day; wonderful things are going to happen today!" You can't stay down-hearted for long when you live with a bundle of optimism. Jan also has a special concern for me that he carries daily to the Lord. It feels good when you know someone is praying for you.

But I'm also willing to reach out to others for

encouragement. That's why I'm so glad God has provided Christian co-workers and a church family to nurture and sustain me. Sometimes when there's an important meeting in the offing, or a key decision coming up, I'll ask a colleague to pray for me.

My friends are especially important. I need all possible energy to get through my long list of daily tasks. The counter-forces of unhappiness, discouragement, and negativism deplete my energy and make me tired. So I choose my closest friends with care: optimistic people. I need every one of them; when I'm experiencing a low I'll give someone a call. We may not discuss my problem; just their cheerfulness and enthusiasm gives me the boost I need.

I encourage them to call me. I constantly pray that I'll correctly read their message and never discourage them when they need help.

Do something loving for someone else. This is another way I help God fill my cup. You see, love has a mysterious property. You can't give it away without getting it back.

So think about those who need love and attention more than you. Whose life could you touch with a little sunshine and happiness? Perhaps you could pick a bouquet of flowers, bake cookies or bread for a neighbor, or send a note of appreciation.

This way of filling your own cup works especially well when you are feeling unloving toward someone. Instead of following your first impulse, turn the leaf and do something nice for him or her.

What could you do for the children who wrote on the wall, messed your closet, and broke your vase? Perhaps you could write them love notes, clean their rooms, or serve a loving message with a piece of pie. Or better yet, give them some of your precious time.

A father once related a story about his teenage son who had hardly spoken for months. They lived in the same house, but communication was almost non-existent. The son was punishing his father with silence. Whenever the father tried to get him to speak, matters became worse.

The father found a ten-speed racing bike on sale. His son had always wanted one, but it was something that he had never felt necessary. Suddenly, an impulse! Why not buy it? He did.

When the son saw the bike, he asked coldly, "Whose bike?"

"Yours," the father replied.

His son was dumbfounded. "For me? Why? I don't deserve a bike!"

"It's yours just the same."

The boy was overwhelmed with his father's kindness. His resistance collapsed., He couldn't contain his feelings. He ran to his father and hugged him. The strike was over.

As the father told the story, he admitted it might have been an illogical thing to do. But it was an effective means to fill his son's love cup. By showing love he reaped a bountiful harvest.

You can be effective in filling your own love cup if you reach out to God and to others and accept the love they are so willing to give. "Ask and you shall receive" is good advice. But don't forget another truth: "Fill another's love cup and you shall be filled."

10

A Life Worth Living

Cliff started life with the same chance as most other children. A mother, a father, a healthy body, fine potential, and a love cup ready to be filled. His problem: finding someone to fill it.

Cliff was a shy, sensitive boy. He was in second grade when his world began to crumble. His parents, whom he loved, were getting a divorce. He was sad and hurt. He became so depressed that he couldn't keep his mind on his teacher's words. The print in his book seemed blurred and the numbers on the page didn't add up. His teacher was concerned. She saw that Cliff was falling behind his classmates. She approached him gently. "Cliff, how can I help you?" Without thinking, she added, "You know, you're the slowest child in the class." She meant only to be helpful, but her careless words staggered Cliff. Now he had to deal both with conflict at home and failure at school.

His classmates all seemed happy and bright. At least so it seemed to him. They quickly picked up ideas which his troubled mind was slow to absorb. He felt left out and alone. He withdrew.

Cliff was afraid to make friends; afraid of rejection. To him it seemed safer just to wait for someone else. He waited. But no one said, "Hi, Cliff. Come play with me."

Cliff never invited anyone to his house. He knew what might happen. His mother had remarried; his stepfather drank heavily and Cliff never knew what to expect. He certainly couldn't explain this to a playmate. Instead, Cliff silently complied with his stepfather's orders. Cliff resented the man. He would have liked to spend more time with his mother, but she, too, was usually hustling to meet the stepfather's demands.

Years passed. Cliff lived in a home devoid of parental affection. His teachers lost interest. He was merely a warm body in the classroom. No one seemed to care.

He was twelve years old when life turned unbearable. One late winter's day he was watching some boys building a snowman. In a feeble voice he asked, "May I help?"

They turned on Cliff like a pack of wolves. They taunted, "Well, if it isn't Cliff Evans! We don't need your help!" One boy grabbed his hat and threw it to his buddy. They played "keep away." Back and forth they threw the hat as Cliff tried to recover it. Finally, the biggest boy pushed Cliff into a snowbank, ceremoniously put the hat on the snowman's head, and named the snowman, "Dumb Cliff."

The same day, Clifford took the long way home, found some pussy willow and arrived late. He thought the pussy willow might please his mother and even his stepfather. Instead, the stepfather was irate. "Where have you been?" he yelled, "I told you to shovel the walk!" He slapped Cliff, knocking the pussy willow from his hand.

The next morning Cliff felt ill. He didn't want to go to school and be teased. He didn't want to stay home and be slugged. Miserable, he boarded the school bus. The kids were happily talking. Everyone else had a friend. He was ignored. They acted as if he didn't exist. Moments later, overcome with pain, he made his way up the aisle and said, "I got to get off!"

The driver yelled at him, "You just got on—I can't let you off!" But at the next stop, he opened the door, Cliff stumbled down the steps and fell down in the snow. Cold. Alone. Empty.

It's a tragic story—documented in Brigham Young University's film, "Cipher in the Snow."

I showed the film to a children's church group. In the discussion that followed, I asked the children, "Is there a Cliff in your school?"

No one answered. Everyone looked at their shoes. Was the silence an expression of guilt? I knew how thoughtless children could be to one another. No doubt most of these had at some time hurt, teased, or ignored another youngster.

I asked again: "Is there a Cliff in your school?"

More silence. At last, nine-year-old Cindy raised her hand. "Yes, it's me," she said in a small voice. "I feel like Cliff every day I go to school."

I couldn't believe it. I had known Cindy for two years. I had been her church school teacher, week after week, and had no inkling of her feelings.

I determined that I would help Cindy. I would fill her love cup and give her hope.

A few weeks later, Cindy's chair was empty. Her family had suddenly moved. No one knew where; there was no forwarding address.

Cindy is out there. There are millions of Cindys and Cliffs stumbling through an indifferent world, waiting for someone to notice them, someone to care, someone to give them hope and a reason for living.

What is it that makes life worth living? A new car? A stylish wardrobe? A video recorder? New wallpaper? Wealth?

You can be short on material possessions, you can lose your wealth, but somehow you'd manage. You can sustain yourself through a famine. You can survive privation in the wilderness. You can overcome persecution, wars, and riots. You can recover from debilitating disease You can live a subsistence life with few material benefits. But you can't live a worthwhile life without meaningful human relationships—ask Cindy.

A loving relationship is basic; more so than wealth, more so than material comforts. Love sustains your hope for something better. With love you can feel good about yourself. Without love there is no hope. Without love you feel worthless.

Regrettably, too many persons suffer from a serious condition: chronically empty love cups. Daily life to them is meaningless. They feel worthless and devoid of hope. This fact is starkly documented by our shocking suicide statistics.

Suicide is the second leading killer among young people 15-24 years of age. And if the underlying cause of many accidental deaths were known, it might possibly emerge as the top culprit. Even young children are not immune. It's the eighth on the list of killers of school-age youngsters. A few decades ago it was almost unknown in this age group.

You might expect the poverty-stricken to choose suicide as a way of escaping an unbearable life; the surprising fact is that affluent teenagers are significantly at risk. The *Wall Street Journal* sought an answer for this problem from the following three professionals.

Dr. Mary Giffin is a child psychiatrist who practices in the prosperous north Chicago suburbs where teenage suicide is epidemic. She has identified a suicide profile. According to her, "Many of the children were high achievers and socially adept, not the sort you usually associate with the act. We can only conclude that we are raising children who have very fragile personalities, kids who can be devastated by the slightest setback."

Dr. Lee Salk, a New York clinical psychologist, said, "The material success of parents can be a detriment to child-raising if it comes at the expense of time that should be spent with their children. Children can tell fairly young what their parents consider important. If they see that everything comes ahead of them, there's likely to be trouble ahead."

Dr. Bennett L. Leventhal, director of the Child Psychiatric Clinic at the University of Chicago Medical School, feels that some parents, being unsure of their own values, are unable to offer their children any goals beyond material success. "The kids perceive their parents' expectations that they'll succeed, but not much else. Too often, they grow up lacking the internal controls they need to keep on course."

What are the factors that cause children to take their own lives? According to these experts, a fragile personality devastated by problems, lack of parental time and attention which engenders a feeling that everything else is more important to parents, and lack of parental guidance to instill worthwhile values and goals.

In a way, these factors can be summarized into one relational need—the need to feel loved. Hand in hand with love is hope—the hope that is with you when your life is filled with love.

When you give of your love, you give time and attention. And love begets love; it instills within the beloved the desire to share love with others. And filling another's love cup is a goal worth striving for! When your love cup is filled, you don't easily succumb to monor setbacks. Love provides a cushion for the rough spots in life. Love permits you to bounce back.

Why not determine that you'll be a love cup filler to your family and friends? As you do, you'll radiate happiness, and in return, your own love cup will be filled to overflowing.

> *"And now abideth, faith, hope,*
> *love, these three; but the greatest of these is*
> *love."*
> *—I Corinthians 13:13*

Conclusion

"May your roots go down deep into the soil of God's marvelous love; and may you be able to feel and understand, as all God's children should, how long, how wide, how deep, and how high his love really is; and to experience this love for yourselves, though it be so great that you will never see the end of it or fully know or understand it. And so at last you will be filled up with God himself." (Ephesians 3:17-19 *The Living Bible)*

When you are filled up with God—when your cup is full—may your love overflow to touch those whose lives touch your own. By experiencing your love, may the unloved become loved and may the lovable be even more loving.

References

1. Kuzma, Kay, *Understanding Children,* Pacific Press Publishing Association, Mountain View, CA., 1978.

2. White, E.G., *Desire of Ages,* Pacific Press Publishing Association, Mountain View, CA., 1940. p. 22.

3. Osborne, Fred, "The Relationship Between the Disposition of Hostility and Non-self-confirming Experiences", (Ph.D. dissertation, The Claremont Colleges, School of Theology) 1972.

4. Schlein, Miriam, *The Way Mothers Are,* Albert Whitman and Company, Chicago, 1963.

5. Chess, Stella, Alexander Thomas and Herbert Birch, *Your Child is a Person,* The Viking Press, Inc. 1965.

6. Dudley, Roger, *Why Teenagers Reject Religion,* Review and Herald Publishing Association, Washington, D.C., 1978.

For information on the Filling Your Love Cup Seminar, seminar materials and other PARENT SCENE seminars, materials, and services write to:

PARENT SCENE
Box 2222
Redlands, CA 92373

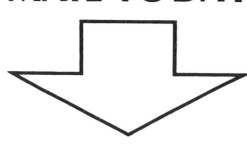

MAIL TODAY

Dear Kay, I enjoyed your book. The three most helpful chapters were:
___1___ ___2___ ___3___ ___4___ ___5___ ___6___ ___7___ ___8___ ___9___ ___10___
As a result of reading this book, I have made a commitment before God
to make the following changes in my life:

_____

Please send me: _____ (put your name and address on opposite side)
☐ Catalog of books and cassettes by Kay Kuzma
☐ Information on Kay Kuzma's seminars
☐ Parent education instructor's materials and training
☐ Information on establishing a Right Beginning Center for parents
   of young children.
☐ A **FREE** issue of the **Parent Scene** newsletter
☐ Send a **FREE** copy of the newsletter and a special offer for this book to
   my friend:
                    Name _____
                 Address _____
                         _____

Name

Address

PARENT
SCENE

Box 2222
Redlands, CA 92373

attn: Kay Kuzma

Place
Stamp
Here